HIS HAND

ON ME

The Road to Kennesaw

Lois Prayor Williams

HIS HAND ON ME: The Road to Kennesaw

Scriptures used are from the King James Version

NOTE: Some of the real names of the individuals contained within this biopic account were changed to protect their privacy.

ISBN: ISBN-13: 978-0-9994252-8-2

Inspired 4 U Publications
http://www.howtoselfpublishinexcellence.com

DEDICATION

I dedicate this book to my parents and their legacy, my sister, and my sons:

To my father, James Edward Prayor, thank you for instilling in us the values we needed to get through life. Thank you for always coming home at night and for keeping our family together through it all.

To my mother, Annie Lou Giles Prayor, your love and strength for your family allowed you to endure and manage the illness of schizophrenia for as long as you did. Thank you, Mama. You are Gone, but Not Forgotten. We Love You!

To my sister, Brenda Yvonne Prayor, although you also had schizophrenia, you were fearless and a writer of poetry. We miss you and will forever cherish your memory.

To my three wonderful sons, Phillip, Anthony Jr., and Alexander, your mere existence gave rise to mine, and I am so proud of the young men that each of you are becoming.

Table of Contents

PROLOGUE... i

INTRODUCTION 1

GROWING UP IN NEW YORK...................................... 3

    The Fire... 7

    Living on Rutland Road 8

    The Walk Home 12

    Reflections 13

PREPARING FOR COLLEGE 15

    The Day I Ran 16

    Meeting Brother Frank...................................... 20

GIVING UP.. 25

MY FIRSTBORN... 35

    Car Troubles.. 37

THE UNTHINKABLE HAPPENED 41

THE MOVE TO BINGHAMTON 49

    Walking On Egg Shells...................................... 51

God Motivated Me to Wear My Seatbelt 54

GETTING MY ASSOCIATES DEGREE...................... 59

Reflections 65

THE MOVE TO TAMPA, FLORIDA 67

Tulsa, Oklahoma 73

THE DAY I STOOD UP... 77

THE DEATH OF A MARRIAGE AND A MATE 85

Reflections 90

APPLYING TO KENNESAW 93

FINAL REFLECTIONS 99

MY PARENT'S LEGACY 101

ABOUT THE AUTHOR 103

WORKS CITED 105

PROLOGUE

During the fall semester of 2016, Dr. Felicia Mainella, my Foundations of Leadership class professor, assigned us to write about two of our life-changing events. I wrote the last sentence of that paper as follows:

"If I ever write a book on my life, I would title it *The Road to Kennesaw* because it has been one heck of a journey."

"The LORD *will perfect that which concerneth me: thy mercy, O* LORD, *endureth for ever: forsake not the works of thine own hands.*

– Psalm 138:8

INTRODUCTION

I finished high school and started college a year ahead of schedule. The fact that I graduated *41-years later* was only by the grace of God. You may wonder what happened.

Life happened.

Initially, when I first thought about writing this book, I was going to name it *The Road to Kennesaw*. It would highlight the traumas that I experienced by the time I entered Kennesaw State University. However, as I was finishing the book, I realized that the title was not a comprehensive depiction of what my life had been about, so I made it my subtitle.

My life had seen its share of traumas by the time I arrived in Kennesaw, GA; yet, interwoven between each experience was a loving God who made His presence known. God showed me that I was not alone, and in honor of His Sovereignty to show up in my life, I thought *His Hand On Me* would be a more suitable title.

Kennesaw was unforeseeable when I dropped out of Binghamton University. But after my marriage ended, and two out of my three children were grown, I became reacquainted with myself and added 'Return to College' on my bucket list.

When my youngest son entered high school, I told myself *if I'm going to do this, I'd better get started*.

I was 52 years old.

Chapter 1

GROWING UP IN NEW YORK

My parents, James and Annie Lou Prayor, were both born in Georgia. They were married in the south but left soon after to move in with my mother's aunt in Detroit. Their eight children, four sons and four daughters, were born up North. But our stay in Detroit didn't last long.

Denise was the first of us to enter the world, and two years later, I made my appearance. By the time I turned two, my parents had pulled up roots and moved us to Queens, New York.

We lived in Queens with Uncle Woody, my father's only brother. The one memory I have of living there is sitting in a chair and screaming. My father told me that I had seen a rat, and 'that was all she wrote'; they had to come and rescue me.

We eventually got our own home in Freeport, Long Island (LI). My first school was Bayview Avenue, where one of the few times I got in trouble occurred. I remember playing jump rope on the school playground, and a boy kept jumping in the rope while we were turning. My playmates and I kept yelling at him to stop, but he wouldn't listen. The next time he jumped in, I yanked the rope out of the other girl's hand. The rope accidentally hit him and left a welt mark on his face. Even though they sent me to the office and called my parents, I still remember feeling justified by what I did.

At this point, all except my last sibling had been born; and for the most part, we had a pretty normal childhood. We lived in a huge white house on Lillian Ave. with a big yard that required a lot of raking in the fall. We would rake up the leaves, jump in, and then have to rake them up again. We caught lightning bugs and put them in jars. We also played hide and seek with Lady, our German Shepherd. We would cover ourselves with a blanket while on the couch, and Lady would nibble at us through it. It stills makes me laugh when I think about how she played with us.

We were very close to three families on our block, the Fallon's, the Addys', and the Tyler's. I can still remember how we laughed and played together. One of the families had a daughter named Mary, who pierced my sister's and my ears. She did it the old fashion way by first pressing an ice cube against our earlobes to numb them; times have surely changed. Although they were Caucasian, they were family. We always played together and shared our food. Mary also had a brother named Billy. What I wouldn't give to see any one of them again.

I must have been about seven years old when we went to the State Hospital to see my mom. I remember her waving to us through the black steel bars. We were not allowed to go in, so my father brought her to the window. We waved to her and told her we loved her.

When momma was in the hospital, two ladies would come to the house to cook, clean, and do the laundry while my Pops was at work. It's been decades since that time, yet I still remember their names, Ms. De'Voe and Ms. Luther. They wore light blue uniforms with beige stockings and soft leather shoes. Even after mom came home, the ladies continued to work.

I remember buying penny candy at the corner store– *penny candy, indeed a thing of the past*.

I was nine years old when I heard momma yell upstairs to my father. "James, they shot King!" Her voice sounded as if it was someone very close to the family. I remember wondering, W*ho is King?*

It was April 4, 1968, the day someone assassinated the Rev. Dr. Martin Luther King Jr. My mother's birthday was the next day.

The Fire

I was eleven years old when the fire occurred. Denise, Yvonne, Ann, and I were all in the back bedroom when someone yelled, "FIRE!" When we opened the door, we saw the fire had spread to the hallway. We slammed the door and heard our father calling us from outside. Dad was yelling for us to jump out of the window. My sisters jumped first, and dad safely caught them, one by one. He caught me also, but ironically I wound up with a busted lip.

God sure was with us that day. Mom was nine months pregnant and in front of the fire, so she was able to walk down the stairs. Dad was home and able to coax us into jumping out the window. We still had each other even though we lost everything, and my baby brother Phillip was safely born the following month.

Unfortunately, our family had to split-up on the night of the fire. Our parents stayed with one neighbor while the boys and girls stayed elsewhere. The firemen concluded that the cause of the fire was electrical. The damage was so extensive that we never returned home.

In our next and final family home, we rented the main floor of a house that was occupied by two other families. The main floor consisted of three bedrooms. My siblings and I shared two of the bedrooms, one for the four boys and the other for the four girls. Each room had two bunk beds, which meant that each of us shared a bed with a sibling. We learned how to make the best use of a small space. The thought of it makes me laugh now.

Several years passed before the other families moved out, and we had the entire house to ourselves. This house was near the elevated train tracks on Rutland Road in Freeport, New York.

Living on Rutland Road

The move to Rutland Road was one of the best things that could have happened to me. It turned out that another eleven-year-old girl lived right next door to where we moved. Her name was Donna, and her family had just moved there about three months earlier. Donna and I became the best of friends. We jumped rope together almost every day and soon became double-dutch partners.

Forty years have come and gone since the days of Rutland Road, yet Donna and I have managed to remain the best of friends. By the grace of God, We have weathered many storms of life together. She is a kind-hearted person, and I am ever grateful to have her in my life.

Despite mom's illness, she had lucid periods in her life that allowed her to interact with us. One of the things she did, during those moments, was baking mouthwatering cakes. She taught me how to bake a cake from scratch, using the blue packaged Pillsbury Best 'Doughboy' Flour. Mom's cakes were finger-licking good. I'll always remember the double-decker coconut cake she baked for my 16th birthday. It was beautiful to look at and scrumptiously delicious. As the saying goes,

"She did that!"

Most of the time, momma would be in her room when I got home from school. It turned out that the doctors had diagnosed her with schizophrenia. The illness caused her to hear voices and think that people on the television were talking about her. So whenever she passed through the living room to get to the bathroom, she put her fingers in her ears to shut out the voices. Schizophrenia kept my mother from going to the Parent-Teacher Conferences and doing any kind of shopping. At the age of 12, I became one of the first girls on Long Island to deliver papers for Newsday, according to my manager. I guess that makes me sort of a trailblazer. I started delivering newspapers thanks to my girlfriend Tanya, who came up with the idea and talked me into it. Yet, Tanya only kept her route for about a week while I kept mine for three years.

Working a paper route led to amazing results: I bought two 10-speed bikes with my money and met Steven, my high school sweetheart. I also rode a horse for the first time during my visits to a Dude Ranch on two separate occasions. I told myself that I would own a horse one day. My father said that having a paper route brought me out of my shyness. All in all, it worked out well for me.

It turns out I was also a pretty good student. I liked counting the many Os that stood for Outstanding on my report card. I remember the time my father came to my junior high school for a parent-teacher conference, and my math teacher Mr. Porzio told him that I was college-material. From that point on, I think I knew that I was going to college.

I had always desired to be either a teacher or a nurse. I also played the flute in the concert band and the piccolo in the marching band. I enjoyed music a lot and experienced a well-rounded childhood. My activities and studies distracted me from focusing on my mom's illness. By all accounts, our family was quite common. We had a father, a mother, a dog, and a house with a white picket fence.

The Walk Home

Looking back over my life, I realize that God was watching over me long before I began my relationship with Him. On one such occasion, I was about 12 years old, walking home alone near the railroad station. I was walking on the curb as if it were a balancing beam. It was something I always enjoyed doing. I approached a stretch of land that consisted of a grassy knoll, a chain-link fence, a parking lot, and then a sidewalk, where I saw someone I knew.

While talking to the person I had recognized, a maroon Cadillac slowly pulled up alongside me. I never bothered to turn my head or acknowledge the person in the car, and then the car pulled away.

I continued to walk towards home through a dirt path that led directly to my street. I've always felt comfortable on this path, so I had no worries. However, once I got to the end of the walkway, I saw the maroon Cadillac again. I dared not cross the street to my house. Fortunately, I was able to cut through the backyard of the corner house. I rang the bell and banged on the door, hoping with all my might that someone would answer. The Cadillac drove around the corner and, like me, waited to see if anyone would come to the door. An *angel* opened the door, and the car drove away.

Reflections

What amazed me about the walk home was the fact that I had seen someone I knew across that grassy knoll, through the chain-link fence, across the parking lot, all the way to the sidewalk and just before the maroon Cadillac pulled up alongside me.

The second amazing thing was that the other person was enough to discourage the guy from grabbing me.

The third thing that amazed me was the man's determination to abduct me. He followed around the corner and waited to see if anyone would come to the door.

"Blessed be the Lord, who hath not given us as a prey to their teeth. Our soul is escaped as a bird out of the snare of the fowlers: the snare is broken, and we are "escaped."

– Psalms 124: 6-7

Chapter 2

PREPARING FOR COLLEGE

I was in line to be the first of my family to go to college. My older sister Denise had never felt inclined to go, and neither of my parents had finished high school.

In high school, I attended Regent classes that were said to be College Prep classes. I remember frequently staying up late to finish my homework, which I was unable to start until I completed my paper route and ate dinner.

I graduated from Freeport High School in August 1976 and enrolled in the State University of New York (SUNY) at Oneonta the same month.

The Day I Ran

My father drove me to the college campus that August in our old station wagon. I remember pulling up to Phillipe Hall, the big grey stone building where I would be living. I went to my assigned room and discovered I had two pretty cool roommates, Gwen and Kathy. Gwen loved make-up, and Kathy loved cats. They were both friendly, and we all got along easy enough.

I went to register for my classes a few days later only to discover that Oneonta did not offer the area of study I wanted to major in. I immediately lashed out at my high school guidance counselor, questioning why she would recommend this school to me if it didn't offer the degree I desired. Although, in all fairness to her, it was just as much my responsibility as it was hers.

Everything happened so quickly once I found out that I could accelerate and graduate a year early. When I informed my guidance counselor that I was interested in going to State schools, she thought it was an excellent idea for me to apply. She hurriedly presented colleges to me, and in equal haste, I applied to them. In our rush to get everything done expeditiously, we neglected to verify if my degree program was a part of Oneonta's curriculum. In any case, maybe this was part of God's plan, a reason for this stop on my *Road to Kennesaw*.

Well, Plan B was for me to take Liberal Arts courses that I'd probably have to take no matter what school I attended. Then I'd transfer at the end of the semester to Binghamton University, which had a School of Nursing curriculum.

Six weeks into classes, a Jewish holiday rolled around, giving us a three day weekend. In learning that many of the students were going home, I decided to jump on the bandwagon and check the campus Ride Board for a chance to get a ride home. I lucked up and caught a ride with a student driving down to New York City.

I was so happy to see my parents and siblings again. It had been my first time being

17

away from them for so long. My mom and I shared a very private moment while I was home; nevertheless, my visit passed all too quickly. When it was time for me to return to school, I remember pausing just before I got into the car. I felt completely helpless, looking at mom as she stood in the front door. "I love you," I told her.

Two days later, while I was in my dorm room, I got the call from my sister. "Lois, mom's dead." "Stop lying, I just saw mom," I responded in disbelief. Then my aunt got on the phone to verify mom's death and tell me to come home. I immediately dropped the phone and took off running without any explanation or destination in mind. I couldn't absorb that news standing still.

When I finally ran out of steam, I decided to go into town and drown my sorrows with alcohol. I ended up in a bar with a jukebox and found the song "She's Gone." I played the song and ordered a drink. I didn't finish it, but I did process the news that my mom was gone.

Mom had ended her own life by walking into the Reservoir. My 12-year old brother Antwan and the baby of the family, 6-year old Phillip, went with her for a walk. Mom walked into the water when they weren't watching. They were unable to reach her, and she drowned.

I took the campus bus back to the dorm, where my roommates were waiting to console me. They had picked up the phone and found out what had happened. Soon after, I rode the Greyhound bus to New York City. I remember looking out the window in a daze and my boyfriend picking me up from the Port Authority Bus Terminal. My life had just changed forever, and I didn't have a clue as to what I was going to do.

I felt a cold chill in the air as I got out of the car and entered the house. Family, friends, and neighbors were there consoling my father. I embraced him. He hung his head down and shook it incredulously. "We were together 18 years," he said before shaking his head again, saying, "Oh my God."

My siblings and I decided to wear brown for the funeral. We were all on one accord in refusing to wear black. It was our way of snubbing our noses at death. There was nothing else we could do, so we did that. We wore brown.

I started toying with the idea of not returning to school, which didn't sit well with anyone. Everyone told me that mom would have wanted me to go back. I decided to return and was quite surprised at the feeling of gratitude that filled me as I drove away from the house. I was lucky to be able to leave. I felt sorry for the others because they had to stay. As I drove away, I realized that I had somewhere to go, a place to escape. The spirit of death was now residing where love and normalcy once abided.

Meeting Brother Frank

I ended up with incompletes in most of my classes that semester, which pushed back my transfer to SUNY Binghamton. The spring semester at Oneonta came with a different roommate, who was also from Long

Island. Her name was Eula, and she was as unique as her name. Two incidents regarding Eula occurred and will always stand out in my memories.

The first incident was when Eula stood up to her boyfriend's roommate. One night I stopped by their room looking for her. I knocked on the door, and the roommate told me to come in. I entered thinking nothing of it because we were familiar with one another. "I'm looking for Eula," I said after I stepped inside. He then let me know that neither she nor her boyfriend was there. I noticed that he was drunk when he shifted his full attention to me. He was looking at me as if I was a T-bone steak, and he hadn't eaten in days. I quickly realized that he was not going to take 'NO' for an answer when he blocked the door as I turned to leave. So I tricked him into thinking that I was willing to have sex with him after all. When he moved away from the door, began to undress, and had his pants off, I made my getaway. I ran out of the room and right into Eula. I told her what had happened, and she became furious. She stormed to our dorm room and grabbed a butcher knife before charging back to say, "If you ever lay a hand on Lois again, I will kill you!"

The second incident changed my life forever. It happened the summer before I transferred to Binghamton University. I went to work with Eula, on Long Island, at an older woman's home. Brother Frank, a visiting minister, came to pray for the lady. My parents had never taken us to church and never went for themselves. So when Brother Frank began to talk to Eula and me about Adam and Eve's disobedience and God's plan to restore humanity to Himself, it all sounded like 'Good News' to me. Brother Frank then asked Eula and me if we wanted to accept Jesus Christ as our Lord and Savior. Eula said no. But I said, "Yes!"

I don't know why Eula said no, and oddly enough, we never discussed it. I, on the other hand, didn't see any reason not to accept Jesus. God only wants a personal relationship with us. That spiritual encounter was the beginning of my relationship with God, which is also the subject of my next book. It will be an audiobook of short stories about how God showed up for me. For instance, "The Walk Home" encounter with the maroon car. The audiobook will come in a paperback format as well.

Later that evening, Eula and I took the train to the Bronx to meet up with some of her friends. On the ride there, Eula started using profanity. Ordinarily, I would have been right there with her. But for some spiritual reason, it bothered me now. I asked her to watch her mouth, and she gave me the strangest look before sarcastically responding, "Gawdly Lois." I nonchalantly shrugged my shoulders. After that, Eula started apologizing whenever she slipped up around me.

My change was unexplainable; I couldn't if I tried. It was what it was.

"And let us not be weary in well doing: for in due season we shall reap, if we faint not."

– Galatians 6:9

Chapter 3

GIVING UP

I arrived at SUNY Binghamton during the fall of 1977. This campus was much bigger than Oneonta's. I met Dwayne outside the campus Post Office when I went to identify my post office box. Dwayne was a pleasant but much older guy, who without exaggeration, literally pounced on me. Nonetheless, we exchanged information, and so began our friendship.

I completed my prerequisites and applied to the School of Nursing. I was overjoyed when I got accepted in the fall of '78. I finished my first nursing class and thought I had done okay. Yet, I had to meet with the Nursing Instructor to find out if I had passed the course and would be allowed to take Nursing II in the spring. The Instructor said, "I don't think you are Head Nurse material. I believe you would be better suited for a 2-year program."

I was heart-broken but equally determined not to let her opinion dictate my future. I also realized there was no reason to stay for the spring semester since the school was not offering the Nursing I course I needed to retake. I decided to take the spring semester off so I wouldn't waste my grant money. However, that one semester off turned into 18 months, and I eventually wound up back home.

I was 17 years old when momma died. At 20-years old, I was living back home in her house for the first time since her death. I remember thinking that I didn't want to be responsible for my life. I didn't want to die, but I didn't know how to live without her. I was depressed. At this point, I was going through life fumbling in the dark, scared, and feeling all alone.

I remember thinking that becoming a prostitute might be the answer. I thought I could get through life having sex with strangers and allowing a 'pimp' to call the shots. *Yep, that's what I'll do. I will go down to 42nd Street and start my new life in the spring.* But, as God would have it, I was out and about one day and saw a pimp beating a young girl. I was horrified and said, "Nope, that's not what I want!" Oh, but for the grace of God, who didn't allow me to go down that path. "Lord, I wholeheartedly thank You!"

Another reason I ended up back home was an attempt to help my father with the remaining five kids. My father had always been a hard-working man. When we lived in Detroit, he once told us that he would not eat before going to work because it wouldn't leave anything for us. I found it commendable that my father would go to work without eating and that he always went to work, and faithfully came home every night. No one can take that away from him.

I never saw my father drunk or behave in

any disrespectful way until I returned home on leave from school. The best way to preface this story is to say that my father inherited a lot of responsibility after my mother died. He worked all day and then came home to take care of four boys and one girl. My father was only too pleased to have me back at home. A typical scenario would be him passionately telling me something one of the kids did. In turn, I would show a great deal of empathy and agree with him that my sibling was wrong. He'd then tell me to go and handle that situation. I remember feeling betrayed and setup.

One day, I got an epiphany. I realized that my father needed help with the children, but that this was not my responsibility. I knew that I could not be a mother to my remaining five siblings and that I no longer wanted to stay at home. I called SUNY Binghamton and asked them what was required for me to get back in school. They sent me a form to complete, which started the process of my return to college.

I went back to school with a fresh determination to succeed. Dwayne had graduated while I was on leave. He had also traveled to some pretty exciting places and sent me postcards from a few of them. We started dating after I returned.

It was Thanksgiving when I noticed that I was having pains in my stomach like nobody's business. I told Dwayne, and he asked me if I wanted to go to the hospital. "No," I told him, even though I felt as if my pancreas or some other organ inside me had burst. The next day, I went to the campus infirmary. The doctor asked me if my cycle had come that month. "No, but it is coming," I said. He suggested I take a pregnancy test to be safe. I received the test results before I left. It was positive. I was pregnant.

I left the office, wondering where I went wrong. *I thought I understood my cycle and had done everything right. I thought I knew how the rhythm method worked. I thought there were only two days of the month that I could get pregnant. I thought I had it mastered. I was wrong. Now I'm 4-weeks pregnant.*

According to the doctor, my due date was July 17. Weeks passed as I contemplated my next move. I felt helpless. My mom was gone. *How was I going to go to school and take care of a child?* I told my father and friends, and they suggested abortion or adoption as possible options. Although I said I'd consider them, neither appealed to me very much. I didn't want to abort my baby, nor did I want to spend the rest of my life wondering where my child was. Nevertheless, I told my father that I would consider adoption, and we left it at that.

I had to withdraw from college again. I was spent and said, "I give up."

Giving up was the frustrated outcry of a young girl with a dream that the circumstances of life kept forcing her to put on hold. First, Mom's death, then the failure in nursing school, and now this. Upon learning that I was pregnant and would have to withdraw from college again, I threw up my hands, and without any reservations, said, "I Give Up!"

Of course, I wanted to finish college, but I did not see any way I could navigate this situation. I felt as if I had one option only. I had to have my baby.

Dwayne's friends thought that because he was such a good catch, he should have a DNA test done to determine if the baby was his. Dwayne's detached and doubtful disposition and non-existent financial support were painful for me throughout the pregnancy. However, the paternity test proved what I already knew– Dwayne was indeed the father.

After being home for a short period, something unexpected and quite disturbing happened. My father approached me and said, "I have raised eight kids, and my nerves ain't gonna be able to take a crying child." He shook his head the whole time he was talking. I was heartbroken, but remember going down to the basement and talking to God. *God, I don't want to be a burden to my father. I need You to make-a-way for my baby and me.* Although I didn't know how God was going to do it, I knew if anyone could, it would be Him.

About a week had passed when my sister

called me about a notice she read on the advertisement board in the laundromat. The ad was from a mother looking for someone to help her with her school-aged son in exchange for room and board. I excitedly told Denise, "This is the answer to my prayer!"

I contacted the young mother, and within days, baby Phillip and I moved in. We were now living in Roosevelt, New York, one town over from Freeport. We stayed with this young mother until two weeks before my delivery date. Afterward, I moved in with Audrey, a friend of mine who lived in Westbury, New York, which was also on Long Island. She allowed me to stay with her so that she could help me while I gained my strength back after the birth of the baby.

Early one morning, I went to Audrey to tell her that my water broke, went back to my room, and got in bed. In a matter of minutes, Audrey was fully dressed. When I asked, "Where are you going?" She said, "To the hospital." Since I wasn't having contractions, I told her, "I'm not going to the hospital."

With a serious expression and a matter-of-fact tone, she said, "You ain't staying here!" It still makes me laugh when I think about how she said that. Rest in Peace (R.I.P), Audrey.

When we got to the hospital, they kept me because my water had broken. However, my baby wasn't born until the next day. How ironic that my healthy 6 lbs 10 oz baby boy was born on his exact due date.

A remarkable thing happened after I brought him home from the hospital. I would be up all night sleepwalking, trying to comfort him when he was crying. And as long as I was standing up, he was quiet and content. But, as soon as I sat down, he would start crying again. I remember saying in drowsy disbelief, "how can you know this!? You are only a baby."

"But my God shall supply all your need according to His riches in glory by Christ Jesus."

– Philippians 4:19

Chapter 4

MY FIRSTBORN

I was now a single mother who couldn't afford an apartment. So I rented a room in the house of an older woman, who also lived in Westbury, LI. I took Phillip to church with me regularly. One night, when he was about four months old, I let him sleep in the bed with me. I will always remember God waking me up in time to see Phillip sitting on the edge of the bed facing me. In one split second, I reached out and grabbed him before he could fall.

I started working when Phillip was about a year old. He was a good child. The lady that we lived with was from Jamaica, West Indies. She was completely independent and strong-willed. God used her to bless us on several occasions. One memorable incident that comes to mind was when I was low on money. She would jokingly tell Phillip, "A man should always have money in his pocket to take the ladies out," and then she would put a bill in his little pants pocket. *Whew! Thank you, Jesus, for that much-needed money. It will carry me through to payday.* This same scenario happened at least three or four times during the two years we lived with her. God always made-a-way for Phillip and me.

Phillip grew into an intelligent child. He stayed in daycare while I was at work and proved to be a natural leader. The daycare provider once told me that Phillip would stand on the steps like a choir director, and all the kids would gather in front of him to sing songs. What amazed us both was that at only two years old, even the older kids followed him.

When Phillip was four years old, I brought him his first drum set; and I can proudly say that he is now a skillful drummer who plays beautifully.

It was only Phillip and me for the first seven years. One of my pleasant memories, during that time, is when we walked home from church – Tabernacle of Faith in Freeport on a beautiful summer day simply singing and having fun.

Today, Phillip has a successful award-winning sales career. He is the number one person that the other competitive sales representatives strive to beat. I mention this because his leadership trait revealed itself when he was only two years old, leading the children in songs at the daycare.

Car Troubles

When Phillip was two years old, we lived in Roosevelt, LI., and I drove an old Dodge Dart car that someone had given me. It drove well, but the brake system needed work; and although I was able to support Phillip and myself, there wasn't any money left over for car repairs. The $30 a week child support I received usually amounted to $60 - $120 at a time.

Despite my car troubles, I noticed a blessing that whenever I used my brakes, there was always enough space to stop my car in front or to the side of me. I needed the extra space because my master cylinder needed replacing. I took the Meadowbrook Parkway to work, and God amazingly always allowed space for me whenever I had to stop suddenly.

One day when I was driving locally, I thought my portion of God's grace had finally run out. I was on a two-lane street, and steady traffic was moving in both directions. When the traffic halted suddenly, I realized that I was going to hit the car in front of me because there was not enough room for me to stop in time. However, as I approached the vehicle in front of me, it moved up in time to provide the space I needed to stop my car. I shook my head in awe at what just happened, knowing the person in front of me would never realize how close he came to being rear-ended. God was still making-a-way for me and was about to show up again in a significant way.

I had already researched how much my car repairs would cost and was stunned when I went to the mailbox and saw a check for $420 from the Child Support Unit. I leaned my head against the house, patted it with my hand, and said, "Thank you, God, for Your provision." The payment was enough for me to get my brakes fixed finally. I felt as if they had held the money in a savings account, and when the amount was enough for what I needed, they released the check. I needed to get my brakes fixed, and that's what I did!

Another car issue arose when a police officer pulled me over for a tail light being out, and I didn't have my registration, license, or insurance card with me. The officer gave me four tickets that day but told me, "If you bring back proof of all the documents, you will only have to pay the fine for the tail light." I went to the police station with the documents and money, but the clerk was unable to locate the tickets. She said, "I would gladly take your money, but can't because there is no record of the tickets in the system." "Thank you for your service," I said and walked out, praising God. God has truly been good to me!

Chapter 5

THE UNTHINKABLE HAPPENED

This story is extremely challenging to tell. I wasn't sure if this chapter would even make the final cut.

I had been celibate for about two years before I started dating again. I had become lonely and wanted to be in a relationship even though my spirit and soul loved the Lord.

Phillip had started kindergarten, and there was a handsome, tall, and lean janitor named Terrence at his school. Terrence and I started seeing each other, and one day, I took notice of his black Monte Carlo car with a burgundy interior. I told him that I had dated a guy in high school with the same type of car, except his car was grey. Terrence told me that his car used to be grey, but he decided to paint it. "I bought it from my cousin's husband, Steven," he said. You could have knocked me over with a feather. Steven was my High School Sweetheart. He used to be the love of my life, and he spoiled me rotten.

At the time, I didn't know I would look back on those days with envy. There will always be young ladies and women who will wish to experience the things I experienced with Steven. We went out to the movies and dinner often. He would always buy me chocolates and cards for Valentine's Day, and balloons and gifts for my birthday. I will always reflect on that relationship fondly and feel so fortunate that I was able to experience those things when I did in my life. I am very aware of the fact that not everybody does.

Anyway, the day came when Terrence and I broke up. The holidays were upon us, and I had gotten a babysitter for Phillip. I was missing Terrence (R.I.P) and decided to catch a cab and go over to his house even though it was late. However, when I got there, I decided not to ring the doorbell. I thought about how his parents would look at me for arriving at such a late hour. I had not met them and wanted to make a better first impression.

I got back in the cab and went to the Hempstead Bus Terminal. I decided that I would catch the Jamaica bus into the city. I had previously met a friend who worked as a vendor in the Port Authority Bus Terminal at 42nd Street. I figured I would hang out with him while he worked before I returned home. *I should have done anything other than what I did that night.*

To my surprise, the Hempstead Bus Terminal was empty. It seemed as if all the buses had just left. I did not want to be left there, but I had no more money, and the cab driver made it very clear that if I were going anywhere else, I would have to perform some type of sex act with him to pay the fare. I had to escape his cab quickly to avoid him from touching me.

I found myself in an empty bus station

feeling stranded and extremely vulnerable. It was about midnight when I walked around the corner to a bar and stuck my head inside the door. Then I went in and asked if anyone knew when the next bus was coming. "Where are you going?" a gentleman asked, and I responded, "To Jamaica." He said that he was going my way and would be happy to give me a ride. I looked him up and down, observing that he had on a suit and a trench coat. I assumed that he was probably safe because he was wearing business attire, and thus accepted his offer.

As we exited the bar, he told me that he lived nearby and would only have to walk a few blocks to get his car. "Okay," I said and proceeded to walk with him. We passed by a few drunken men on the sidewalk, and I felt safer walking with this young man in the suit. But suddenly, I experienced an epiphany and no longer felt safe with this professionally dressed man. When I started to put a little distance between us, he said, "My building is just ahead."

We entered the building and started walking up the stairs. Soon after, I felt the barrel of a gun against my head. He said, "If you scream, I will blow your f#@*ing head off. Keep walking." We walked up to another flight, and I realized we could go no further. I don't recall him telling me to undress, but I do remember that the window to my left opened to the roof.

I laid there as he raped me, and I remember asking God a question and then making an urgent request. *Why would you let this happen to me?* God's response was for me to "visualize Jesus on the cross," so I focused on picturing Jesus hanging on the cross. My urgent request was, *Please don't let this man throw me off this roof.*

"I'm sorry," the jerk dared to say when it was over. "I have to get my keys," he said and walked away. We mutually understood that he wasn't coming back. I quickly dressed and then started banging on doors. It wasn't long before someone opened their door. I told them what happened, and they allowed me to come in and use their phone. I called the police, and my sister, and then went to the hospital, where they processed a rape kit.

It's been more than 25 years since that experience, but as I retell it, I still feel some of the pain as if it occurred yesterday. In one of my Literary classes, I learned it's a byproduct of experiencing trauma – that "time stands still" when it comes to the pain and the emotion of it.

His Hand On Me: The Road to Kennesaw is an example of Scriptotherapy, which is a term coined by Suzette A. Henke to define "the process of writing out and writing through traumatic experiences in the mode of therapeutic reenactment" (Andermahr). Under the heading of Traumatic Reenactment, Bloom says that "people who have been traumatized cannot heal themselves alone and for healing to occur, we must give words and meaning to our overwhelming experiences."

Ironically, I was due to return to SUNY Binghamton the following month on January

13, 1989, which I saw as my saving grace. I knew that I could change locations and leave this trauma behind me, and that's what I did.

I was this person, the young lady who left Long Island about three weeks later. It was I who returned to Binghamton, New York, with my seven-year-old son to pursue my BS degree from SUNY Binghamton. I was the young lady, who at age twenty-nine, decided to find a husband so that I would no longer be caught out at midnight looking for love. I was the young lady that a stranger raped. And to think I thought he was safe because he was wearing a suit with a trench coat. I've got to be more careful. I was the young lady who arrived in Binghamton on January 11, 1989.

*"He healeth the broken in heart,
and bindeth up their wounds."*

– Psalm 147:3

Chapter 6

THE MOVE TO BINGHAMTON

I remember the day Anthony and I first met. He was from Philly, and I had recently returned to Binghamton University from New York. At the time, I was applying for food stamps at the Department of Social Services (DSS). Anthony was also there, applying for assistance because his job had fired him due to a holiday misunderstanding. He had assumed that every business was closed for Martin Luther King Jr.'s birthday and did not go to work. He thought he was off that day. He was wrong.

We left DSS that day without exchanging contact information because my worker had called me into her office, and when I came out, he was gone. However, Binghamton was a small city, so I knew that I would most likely see him again.

About three days later, I was on the bus and saw Anthony walking down the street. I got off the bus. He was gorgeous. I figured he must realize how handsome he was, but it turns out he didn't. He was not conceited at all, and with that, he had me. We became inseparable, and I forgot all about school and the reason I had returned to Binghamton. I never registered for the spring semester; instead, I married Anthony two months later.

We figured it was fate that brought us together. We had both just arrived in Binghamton when we met. We had both lost our mothers during our teenage years, which I thought for sure would bond us together forever and make us the perfect couple. I felt that our similar traumatic experience would enable us to understand each other's struggles and pain. But I was completely wrong.

Walking On Egg Shells

I learned that Anthony's childhood had been unfortunate. He, accompanied by his sister, was placed in a loving foster home at the tender age of five. However, his foster parents enrolled him in the Boy Scouts of America, where his scout leader molested him. Anthony kept the molestation to himself but began to act out in inappropriate ways. His foster mom's inability to cope with his negative behavior forced her to place Anthony back in the foster care system. He was separated from his sister and placed in a new foster home, where his foster brother molested him. After Anthony became an adult, he went to prison for burglary and served eight years. I met Anthony after he had done his time and was trying to rebuild his life.

We had only been married a month when I found out I was pregnant, and our new reality began to unfold. The pregnancy was no accident. Anthony had missed out on his first son's childhood and desperately wanted another child. Two months later, I came face to face with Anthony's temper when I innocently laughed at him. He overreacted, saying, "If you laugh at me one more time, I will put your head through that brick wall." *Whoa. How do you forget those threatening words? You don't.*

I attempted to 'get out of dodge' the very next day. However, some well-meaning friends foiled my plan. The idea was for my friend to take me to pick up my son Phillip from school and then drive us to the Greyhound Bus Station. I had no intention of going back home because I felt like I had married a nut. But instead of taking me to the bus station, she drove to her house. Can you come inside for a moment?" she asked. I went inside and saw Anthony there waiting for me.

My dear friend and her husband had made a plan of their own. They had brought Anthony and me to their home, hoping to help us work out our differences and save our marriage. She had 'thrown me for a loop.' I remember telling her, "Remind me not to call you the next time I want to do something."

Eight months rolled by, and our first son was born. We named him after his father. It would be three years before I would try and leave again. Anthony hit me once during those three years. Had I not walked around on eggshells and lived in fear of upsetting him, he probably would have wiped the floor with me daily. But, I made an intentional effort not to make him angry. I tried to give him whatever he wanted and say whatever he needed to hear to maintain peace in our home. For the most part, I only succeeded in creating a prison, and thus made myself a prisoner. I felt trapped in what became a way of life that I was not used to living. But we were a family.

Although I enjoyed the status of being married, I began to resent the fact that I couldn't speak my mind. Anthony and I were forever clashing for one reason or another. We could never get to an understanding of yesterday's disagreement because there was always a different fire to extinguish daily. Our life became a constant cycle of abuse. The domestic violence cycle consists of four phases: Tension Building, Incident, Reconciliation/Honeymoon, and Calm. The Honeymoon Phase of the cycle is what made everything else work. This phase made me believe things weren't all that bad. This phase made me feel like "I can do this." The Honeymoon Phase was the part of the cycle that kept me coming back.

God Motivated Me to Wear My Seatbelt

This incident occurred during the first week of June 1990, when my second son Anthony Jr. was about four months old. We were all living in Binghamton, New York, in a beautiful two-bedroom apartment on the second floor. The house was in the middle of the block at the top of a hill.

As I got in my car and proceeded to go down the hill, I felt this overwhelming urge to fasten my seatbelt. Yes, I was well aware of the annual "Seatbelts Save Lives – Click It or Ticket" campaign and believed it. However, I rarely put my seatbelt on because it was so uncomfortable. But on this particular day, that strong urge to 'Click It' weighed unrelentingly heavy on my mind such that I had to comply and buckle up to get relief. I felt the same uneasiness for several days following and finally shared those experiences with my husband.

The 4th of July followed a week later, and I decided that I wanted to see the fireworks show that evening. My husband declined to go with me, so I invited my friend April, who gladly accepted the invitation. I safely strapped Anthony Jr. in the front seat while April and her four kids sat in the back. After we securely strapped everyone in the car, we proceeded to the area of the fireworks show. I stopped at the gas station for directions because although I was familiar with the area, I was not sure of the exact location. Excited to get there, I eagerly returned to the car and promptly drove away without fastening my seatbelt. As God would have it, I had to stop for a pedestrian before entering the roadway. While waiting for this person, aka 'angel' to cross, I put my seatbelt on like those prior experiences had motivated me to do.

After I had fastened my seatbelt and the pedestrian crossed, I drove a little way and stopped at a red light. I proceeded through the intersection when the light turned green, and a car coming from the opposite direction made a left turn and broadsided me. The vehicle pushed me into a steel pole and instantly propelled me towards the windshield. The seatbelt stopped my forward motion, springing me back into the seat. Still dazed, I got out of the car and checked on my passengers. They were all still in their seatbelts, a bit shaken with some minor bruises, but everyone was okay overall. The car, however, was totaled.

The events of the previous two weeks came rushing back to me, making incredible sense. It was God's grace and goodness, showing up in my life again in a significant way. He knew this day was coming. He knew that the force of hitting that steel pole would propel me into and most likely through the windshield. In His infinite wisdom and unconditional love for me, He strongly urged and repeatedly reminded me to wear my seatbelt so that I would be protected.

Overwhelmed with all kinds of emotions, I thought back to the pedestrian who crossed in front of me, giving me the final opportunity to put my seatbelt on. When I reflect on that incident, I realize that if God had not intervened, it's a strong possibility that I could have died or suffered brain damage, been paralyzed, or scarred for life. But instead, I walked away without a scratch and years later wrote this book, *His Hand On Me: The Road to Kennesaw*.

*"I shall not die, but live,
and declare the works of the Lord."*

— Psalm 118:17

Chapter 7

GETTING MY ASSOCIATES DEGREE

I went back to work doing housekeeping at one of the local hotels when Anthony Jr. was about a year old. I remember coming home one day complaining about something at the job when my husband made a statement that initiated a pivotal moment in my life. "You need to leave that job and go back to school." "How am I going to do that?" and "Who's going to watch the baby?" I asked. To my surprise, he sincerely said, "I will babysit."

I was tired of accumulating college credits with no degree to show for it. I figured that I would go to the Community College just over the bridge from us and compile my credits into a 2-year degree. I applied to Broome Community College in the fall of 1991 and majored in Mental Health. The Mental Health curriculum helped preserve my mental health, in regards to the challenges I had already experienced before and during my marriage. In the two years that it would take to earn my degree, I decided to give Anthony equal time to get his act together and then reassess where we were at the end. With a plan in place, I buckled down and got busy earning my degree.

In the midst of me earning my degree, Anthony and I had another blow-up that led me to seek protection at my first Battered Women's Shelter. Although he had not hit me, he intensely expressed his anger about my unwavering focus on schoolwork. On one occasion, he exhibited irrational behavior while driving with the baby and me in the car. He was supposed to take me to school and then drop the baby off. Instead, he said in a menacing tone, "So you want to make it all about you, huh? I got something for you."

Anthony started driving way beyond the speed limit and drove right pass the college. I earnestly prayed, *Lord, I don't know how you're going to do it, but I know you're going to get me out of this.* And God did!

It was a harrowing experience. Anthony stopped to drop the baby off at the daycare and made him go inside by himself. Anthony had held my arm with one hand and let the baby out of the car with his other hand. The daycare staff knew something was wrong and called the police. I pulled the keys out of the ignition with my free hand and threw them out of the car, which forced him to let go of my hand. I then ran down the street, and with no place to go, I hid under a car.

I agreed to go to a domestic violence shelter. Anthony said that he only wanted to talk, but his behavior frightened me, and I needed to escape. I went to the shelter because I needed to feel safe. In reflection, Anthony probably felt insecure and scared about the future as my graduation date drew near. While this may explain it, it certainly does not justify it.

Time seemed to fly. Before I knew it, it was May 1993, and I was graduating. Anthony threw me a beautiful graduation party that took place about two weeks after that domestic dispute. It turned out to be a pretty nice affair. The food was great, and it was good to be celebrating such a wonderful occasion with my friends.

A month later, another altercation occurred that caused something in me to snap. Out of sheer frustration, I threw my keys towards him. At that moment, I knew I had to get out before someone got hurt. Anthony did not argue the point when I told him I needed some time and was returning to the shelter. My time at the shelter convinced me that I needed to leave him. When I told Anthony that I was not coming back to him, he left for Florida, and I went back home. We separated for three years.

Even though my marriage was anything but healthy, it allowed me the chance to escape from the traumas of my mother's death and the rape. I stopped going to church after I left Anthony. I started a relationship with an alcoholic and subsequently got introduced to the programs of Alcoholics and Narcotics Anonymous. I found both programs to be a great source of comfort to me during that season. However, on one occasion, I met a woman who invited me to be a part of a threesome. I instantly turned down the invitation only to accept it two weeks later.

I had run head-on into some feelings that I did not want to deal with and tried to escape them. *Hmmm, let me call that girl back.* I did, and we indulged. But, in the morning, the wife went after her husband with a butcher knife during a subsequent argument. Someone called the police, and I quietly slipped away.

When the woman first asked me to participate, I remember thinking she must be crazy. I also wondered why another woman or man would invite a third party into their bed. Well, I can tell you as a first-hand witness and participant that it does not end well. And in the running from my pain, I had an agenda also.

Shortly after this incident, all hell broke loose in my life, and I discovered that God uses people and situations to get our attention. Like the prodigal son, I gratefully came back into the fold after a succession of distressing events caused me to rethink the direction of my life. One event came in the form of a phone call telling me that my friend Margaret had been killed by a tractor-trailer while crossing the interstate. She had dropped by my house just three days earlier to say goodbye before leaving on a missionary trip. Two days later, my five-year-old son Anthony Jr. and his friend set his friend's house on fire while playing with a lighter. Thankfully they escaped unharmed, but the fire badly damaged the house. I took it as a frightful, life-changing wake-up call to get my life under control.

I was through running from God. I returned to the church that Anthony Sr. and I had attended together. I was glad to be back. I joined the Helps Ministry and volunteered to pick up anyone who needed a ride to the services. It was at this church that I got delivered from cigarettes. I had gone from being a non-smoker to smoking a pack a day after Anthony and I separated. I told myself that I would stop once the stress let up. However, it took returning to the fold and three years for me to quit smoking.

One day, about three to six months after I had returned to the church, Anthony reached out to tell me about a great church he had joined. So I decided to take the boys to Florida to see Anthony and visit his church.

Reflections

As human beings, there are times when we do not know how to handle pain, so we engage in all kinds of unhealthy activities to numb it. We drink, we drug, we become promiscuous, etcetera. The list is as endless as the problems they create for us. I was no exception.

When Anthony and I separated, I was

right where I needed to be– in God's house, where people I knew loved me and would support me. But I did not consider that at the time. Instead, I immediately sought out ways to numb the pain, and there was plenty of it. It never occurred to me that God had already made provisions for me to heal the pain. All I had to do was stand still and let him love me back to health.

You see, *"The earth is the Lord's, and the fullness thereof; the world, and they that dwell therein"* (Psalms 24:1).

Chapter 8

THE MOVE TO TAMPA, FLORIDA

The church had a terrific outreach ministry. They took in people who had lost their way in life and provided a safe place for them while they learned the word and will of God. I was excited about the work they were doing and happy that Anthony had found such a place. They ministered to me about our family getting back together, and I decided to give it another chance. I knew that it would be different this time because I would not be alone like I had been in the past. The church would be our support system. I decided to stay in Florida.

I found myself more excited about the ministry than I was about my marriage. The outreach ministry developed a travel component as time went on, and some of the men would go out of town to raise money for it. My husband became a natural at fundraising. God seemed to bless him favorably in this area, and I began to travel with him. We would be gone for a month at a time, leaving the kids in the care of a church member.

Our second son Alexander was born in Florida. He was as handsome as the other two. Now, there were three. As time went by, Phillip began to play the drums for the ministry and became a pretty good musician. It became evident that he was accepted as such because they always asked him to play on Sunday mornings whenever the official drummer was late. Philip grew excited at their requests for his presence because it symbolized that he was good enough to sit-in. I was happy for him because he had found his niche.

God blessed Anthony Sr. and I both to do a great-work in Florida. However, there were still times when Anthony's temper and jealousy got the best of him. I don't remember what the arguments were about, but I can recall how fearful I felt when he got angry. We were on the road one day when his anger flared up terribly. The Pastors were indeed my saving grace and were always available for me to call whenever something was going on with us. They were able to help calm Anthony down. Just thinking about how Anthony was with me and how he calmly responded to the Pastors brings a smile to my face. It reminds me of how moms are sometimes forced to yell at their kids to get things done while the father only has to mention it once for their kids to respond accordingly.

In time, we were made Pastors and given a church in Roanoke, VA, where we helped people and won souls. Roanoke was a tiny city that I felt was one of Virginia's best-kept secrets. One highlight of being Pastors was when we were traveling in Maryland with a donation team and met a young man living in the woods. He was standing outside a fast-food restaurant asking for change. A couple of the brethren talked to him and were able to convince him to leave the woods and give the ministry a chance. He was able to get his life back on track. This chance meeting occurred on my birthday, and I felt God had given me a spiritual baby as a birthday gift. It doesn't get much better than that. That young man grew and blossomed. He learned God's word and eventually became a minister, got married, and had at least one child.

Another highlight of the ministry happened when I saw my husband genuinely labor with one of the new souls that came off the street. He sincerely poured his heart out, praying and ministering to that young man. It remains a very proud moment for me as his wife. He was determined to get that young man free that night. Anthony was a good Pastor. Looking back, I don't think I gave him enough credit. I believe that if I could have dug deeper within myself and been more spiritual, then maybe I could have helped him better. However, perhaps that's my co-dependency talking. Thinking that somehow I could control him.

Another highlight occurred with a young man who lived on the streets for many years. We came across him while we were doing a donation drive. We tried for more than an hour to convince him to go back to the house with us. We told him about how we could assist him and wanted nothing more than a chance to help. We were all so thrilled when he finally agreed to let us help. He came home with us that night, bathed, changed his clothes, and ate with us. He got up the next morning and thanked us for all that we had done for him, but said he had lived outside too long and was not able to stay inside. Our joy was short-lived when he left because we felt as if we had failed. We were devastated to see him go.

By God's grace, we were able to sustain the church for two years. However, due to faults of our own, we were not able to maintain it.

I would be remiss if I didn't share the story about the rat. We had moved into a lovely house, but we had to clean it out because the former tenants had left it quite messy. I was upstairs cleaning out a lot of debris and about to tackle a closet full of clothes when my husband called me to come downstairs. We ended up switching places and tasks. A short time passed when he came back downstairs, telling me how a humongous rat ran out when he bent down to start removing the clothes. Wow. God had spared me that frightening sight.

I honestly can't imagine how I would have handled that experience. I saw that rat sometime later when I was about to enter the hallway on my way to the bathroom. I was astonished to see how big he was and was able to grab the doorpost as he ran pass me. I can honestly tell you that I would have been no more good had I uncovered that monster. I kid you not, the size of that rat was equivalent to a huge cat. The goodness of God is incredible. I love Him so much because He always looks out for me. "Thank you, Lord, for sparing me."

Tulsa, Oklahoma

After we left Roanoke, Va. we spent about two years in Tulsa, Oklahoma, with Pastors Ben and Robin Maye (R.I.P) and their church. I mention this because of an incident that happened with Anthony Jr. while we were there. Anthony Jr. went through a brief period as a teenager when he would run away from home. On one such occasion, he had been missing for 2 to 3 days. My husband and I agreed that it was time to look for him and asked God to lead us to where he was.

We went to his usual places, including the hospitals, but were unable to find him. We decided to try the movie theaters and came up empty-handed at the first one. It seemed like quite a bit of time had passed during our search, and my husband mentioned calling it a day. "No," I said, speaking with fierce determination. "We came out to find Anthony, and we have to check that other theatre to see if he is there."

We parked across the street and walked through the door. As we entered, I saw someone step back behind a wall. I continued to walk towards where I saw the person, and wouldn't you know it– it was my son. "How do you think we found you?" I asked him. "God," he said. I replied, "You got that right!" So with our child in tow, we went home. Under normal circumstances, trying to find a runaway teenager is like looking for a needle in a haystack. That's how I felt when we started the search, "*but with God, all things are possible*" (Matthew 19:26b).

It had been quite a journey. I enjoyed collecting donations on the street. We had buckets with lids on them that we would take into the streets when the light turned red like the firemen on Labor Day. While accepting donations one day, I remember being asked, "How does one know that the money is going to the church?" "I have to answer to someone greater than you," I replied. Another response I gave was that I wouldn't do this for myself, and I truly meant that. Soliciting donations was a very humbling experience, but knowing that the money was going to help people made it all worthwhile.

God showed me that He was working with us many times. Like the occurrence on my first day out when I was sitting in front of a supermarket. A lady passed by me and entered the store as if I were invisible. She came out and passed by me again in the same manner. A few seconds later, that same woman came over to me in silence with her head bowed and dropped money in the bucket. I don't know what God said to her or brought to her remembrance. I only know that she was obedient and responded with action. Although it occurred over 20-years ago, its profound impact causes me to remember it as if it happened yesterday.

*"Commit thy works unto the Lord,
and thy thoughts shall be established."*

— Proverbs 16:3

"Why art thou cast down, O my soul? And why art thou disquieted in me? Hope thou in God: for I shall yet praise Him for the help of His countenance."

– Psalm 42:5

Chapter 9

THE DAY I STOOD UP

From Tulsa, Oklahoma, we were sent to help the Pastors in Indianapolis. Indianapolis was where things came to a head for Anthony and me. One day, I was in the basement doing laundry while talking on the phone to my childhood friend Donna. I commented, "all these men in my life," referring to my sons and my husband. However, Anthony overheard the comment and immediately jumped to conclusions. He didn't realize that I was talking about him and our three sons. When I entered the room, he rushed over to me, repeating the phrase "all these men in your life, huh?" while simultaneously punching me in my head. It was only by God's grace that I was able to put my hands up and block his punches from making contact with my head. I was grateful because one blow could have been fatal.

As he swung towards my head in anger, I prayed that God would have mercy on him and forgive him. I knew he had misunderstood and had the conversation all wrong. When he stopped attacking me, I continually tried to get him to understand the context of my comment. We made it through the night without any more altercations.

Morning came, and we dressed to go collect donations. While waiting for our ride to pick us up, Anthony realized that he had jumped to conclusions and apologized. But, I told him that I would not be able to bear much more. Angered by my response, he asked why I felt the need to say that.

It was about six months later when the final incident happened. I had been reading a book called *Codependent No More: How to Stop Controlling Others and Start Caring for Yourself.* I saw it in one of the girls' rooms where I worked and asked if I could borrow it. She told me I could have it. I was excited about reading the book and was amazed at how much I related to the content. It was as if someone had cut me open and spilled my guts out on paper. I felt as if I finally had a name for the illness I knew I had. I was Codependent. According to Melody Beattie, author of *Codependent No More*, "A codependent person is one who has let another person's behavior affect him or her and who is obsessed with controlling that person's behavior."

Our last altercation erupted when Anthony and I were in the bedroom, and he responded angrily to something I said. Repeating a portion of what I said, he jumped up and slapped me in the face. His fingernail caught the corner of my eye when his hand made contact. It was then that I had an epiphany: *He could have put my eye out. Let me get out of this marriage before something happens that cannot be reversed. He and I may know he didn't mean to do it; but, it won't matter because the damage will already be done.* That's when I decided that I'd had enough. His nail making contact with my eye caused me to fully realize that I could no longer stay in our marriage. Once again, I mentally began to make plans to leave.

What happened next was nothing short of a miracle. I left to take Alexander to school, and upon my return, Anthony approached me and said, "I think we need some time apart." I agreed and told him about my plan to leave, but he responded that he would go instead. "You have a better job than I do, and I can't afford this place," he said. He also reasoned that if I stayed, the kids could stay in their schools. I agreed. But then, about two weeks later, while packing to leave, Anthony stopped and said, "I don't know why I'm leaving." That's when I knew I had to speak up.

I had never been so close to being free before. I had waited years for my husband to realize we weren't working well together, and for our marriage to be over. I longed to be free to rediscover my voice. I remember, on more than one occasion, begging God not to let me die this way. I had become someone that I did not recognize. So when he said, "I don't know why I'm leaving," I was too close to freedom to turn back. I found the courage to say, "I know why. You're leaving because I asked you to." Then, I became instantly fearful as soon as I spoke those words. Up to this point, Anthony and I had gotten along reasonably well since we agreed to end our marriage. However, *domestic violence* is all about power and control. Standing up and reaffirming my intent to separate left me feeling very uneasy.

That night, I thought it best to sleep downstairs on the couch to be close to the door if I had to flee. I earnestly prayed that God would keep me safe. Anthony woke me up about 6:00 that morning. In a last-ditch effort, he had called a mutual friend hoping that she could talk me out of separating. But, I would not be moved. I had lost myself long ago, and I wanted nothing more than to rediscover the person I once was. Anthony took his belongings and walked out the door that morning without saying a word. He didn't even bother closing the door behind him.

I spent the day getting my hair done and reliving the events that led up to that day. I was so proud of myself for standing up to Anthony when he questioned why he was leaving. I had spent my entire marriage walking on eggshells around him. But on that last night, I found the courage to stand up for myself, my life, and my freedom.

You could not have told me that I would stay in the same house with my husband while he packed his clothes to leave for good. You could not have made me believe that Anthony would leave peaceably. But that's what happened, and I'll always be grateful to God for allowing this experience. I had spent my whole marriage trying to avoid violent confrontations. I never imagined for a second that a peaceful resolution was possible. I'm still in awe of how it all came about. It was surprising and nothing short of God's grace.

If I consider how unsettling life was for Anthony as a child, I can almost understand how he must have wanted to control the people and circumstances in his adult life, in hopes of having a better outcome. However, happiness comes from allowing people the freedom to be themselves. Control is not a form of love. When individuals have been abused and traumatized, they should seek counseling to help them process those events and give themselves a better chance of experiencing healthy relationships. They owe it to themselves and those that love them. Without professional counseling, traumatized people often traumatize others, and abused people often abuse others. Healing takes time.

I loved my husband, and I truly forgive him for all the pain he caused me. I do believe he loved me and tried to do his best with what he had. He tried to do right by his kids and me. We did not have a healthy marriage, and because of fear, I lost my voice a long time ago. Nonetheless, he fathered two of my sons and became a father to my firstborn. We shared some happy moments, and we even shared some laughs.

I also accept the part I played in our dysfunctional marriage. I was anything but healthy when I met Anthony. I was wounded, battered, and bruised. I had just been raped and had only recently started to deal with my mother's death. I desperately needed time to heal, but in my ignorance, I got married instead.

Unbeknown to me at the time, no one should ever make a life-changing decision like marriage when they have experienced any trauma. The death of a loved one, domestic violence, and rape are only a few traumatic events that require time to heal.

I am pleased to say that I have recently resumed counseling to discuss the issues that I talk about in this book and beyond. I have always enjoyed counseling. Counseling provides guidance and assistance in resolving personal, social, and psychological problems and difficulties. It allows you to set aside time to unwind and discuss all that ails you. It is a form of self-care that can enable you to feel pampered and nourished. I strongly recommend it to all.

Chapter 10

THE DEATH OF A MARRIAGE AND A MATE

Anthony and I never got back together. I tried to find a reason to bridge that gap, but my mind never could. There were too many unresolved issues and too much pain. He was a good guy who never fully recovered from a tragic childhood. In 2005, I decided that his childhood was not my fault and that I could not spend the rest of my life paying for it. We parted amicably, which was a testament to God's Grace in our lives.

We separated on April 29, which I will always remember now because it ironically turned out to be my youngest brother Phillip's birthday. This day came to mind several weeks after Anthony left when I tried to figure out how I could have missed my brother's birthday while waiting for it to arrive. That's when I realized it was the same day Anthony left. I had spent that entire day getting my hair done and reflecting on my marriage.

We had been separated for about two years when Anthony called and said, "I want Alexander to come and live with me." I was stunned. I have to admit I didn't see that coming. I knew what Anthony was asking me, and I replied, "I'm going to miss my son, but you and he need each other." We made plans for Alexander to go live with his father, and for the first time since 1981, I did not have any children at home. It was hard to believe that I had suddenly become an empty nester. Nevertheless, it turned out to be a Godsend. Alexander stayed with his father for three years.

The summer that Alexander came home to visit me, I had no intention of sending him back to his father. What I didn't know at the time was that Alexander had no intention of going back either.

Approximately 18 months after Alexander returned home, I got a call from my oldest son Phillip. It was January 21, 2012, and I was returning from lunch and had not clocked in for work yet. Phillip asked me what I was doing and then told me to clock out for the day. "Why," I asked, but he wouldn't respond. "I will need to give a reason for leaving early." "I'm on my way up there. I'll tell them when I get there." "You're on your way to my job?" "Yes." The way he said "yes" filled me dread. I knew something was wrong. My mind was scattered and racing all over the place as I went to clock in from my lunch break. When I reached the back near my locker, one of the support managers approached me. He informed me that I had a visitor at the Customer Service Desk and that I should clock out.

My tears started flowing as I intuitively knew that someone I loved dearly was either severely hurt or had passed away. My father, who was 82-years old at the time, came to mind first. Then I thought about my siblings. Mom and dad had eight together, and my father also had three with his first wife. The support manager tried to comfort me as we walked toward the Customer Service Desk, but I told him the visitor was my son, and I knew that someone had probably died. When we got to the front of the store, the manager handed me over to my son. We walked out to the parking lot, where Phillip confirmed that someone had died. It was my husband Anthony, the father of my sons.

When death shows up to take your loved one, a fog accompanies it that seems to encompass everything suddenly. I immediately felt transported to this foggy place and resided there, at the very least, until the funeral was over. I experienced this when my mom passed, and here it was again.

I had spent the previous five years trying to divorce Anthony, but it wasn't to be. A drunk driver killed Anthony before the divorce was final. At the time of his death, Anthony and his first love had reunited and were engaged. He lived in Delaware and was on his way to work when God called him home.

The roads were covered over with frost, and Anthony was waiting for the bus when a young drunk driver lost control of his car. At 53-years young, Anthony died shortly after being hit. We buried Anthony in Delaware, where his fiancée and oldest son live. Anthony's fiancée Linda and I made the funeral arrangements together. It was through this experience that we became friends.

Some ironic details surrounded Anthony's death. He was from Philadelphia and had a near-death experience before coming to Binghamton, New York. He had almost died from alcohol poisoning. He told me that he was recuperating in his hospital bed – *possibly dreaming*– when he saw his spirit hovering over his body. It did a 180-degree turn before it went back into his body. "I decided to stop drinking right then and there."

The drunk driver who fatally hit him had driven from Philadelphia to drop someone off and was heading back home when he lost control of his car. Anthony died shortly after being hit. He leaves four sons to mourn his passing along with a whole host of friends and family.

We all miss him and wish he was still here. He left us too soon.

Reflections

Anthony was a good listener who listened to me whenever I was able to open up to him. He also gave me some good advice. I remember the time when I was talking to my neighbor, who did not bother to turn around and acknowledge me while I was talking to him. Anthony politely touched my arm and said, "The man is rude, and if he doesn't have the decency to turn around and talk to you, you should stop talking to him."

One of my fondest memories of Anthony

was during the early days of our marriage when I was pregnant with Anthony Jr. That baby was always lying in a position that painfully triggered a nerve in my leg. It didn't matter how many times I pushed him over in my belly; baby Anthony would still manage to fall back onto that same spot. On this particular day, I was having difficulty walking while on our way to the supermarket. Well, Anthony grabbed a shopping cart and motioned for me to get in. "Huh?" I responded. "Get in, I'm gonna push you," He said. Yes, I did get in and was able to get some relief as he pushed me around in that shopping cart. I shake my head in amusement as I reminisce now.

*"To appoint unto them that mourn in Zion, to give
unto them beauty for ashes, the oil of joy for mourning,
the garment of praise for the spirit of heaviness that
they might be called trees of righteousness, the planting
of the Lord, that He might be glorified."*

– Isaiah 61:3

Chapter 11

APPLYING TO KENNESAW

I had been living in Indianapolis, IN, for about five years when I finally decided to move to Georgia. Philip had moved to Atlanta about five years earlier to establish a relationship with his father. Alexander was in high school, and I was 52-years old. I realized that if I was going to go back to college, I had better get started.

I started inquiring about the schools in my area and decided that Kennesaw State University in Georgia sounded like it would be the best fit for me. I also considered Georgia State, but I didn't trust going downtown for classes. I thought it held a propensity for too many distractions. Oliver, a close friend of mine, took the ride with me to find out what was required to apply to Kennesaw.

The Registrar told me that I had to apply online and pointed me to the computers that I could use to submit my application. It wasn't until I had completed the form that I read there was a $45 processing fee required. I checked my bank account to see how much money I had. Thank God for the $50 balance that was there! Knowing that this was my chance, I took it.

I was ecstatic when I received the acceptance letter. After all these years, I was finally going back to school. I worked full-time while attending school on my days off, thanks to Nitro, my supervisor at the time. Nitro suggested that I take Tuesdays and Thursdays off from work so I could get to my classes on time. Her welcomed suggestion came after I got upset because they hadn't adjusted my schedule in time for me to make it to my first class. "I can do that?" I asked. Yes. You put it in, and I'll approve it. This way, you don't have to worry about getting off in time for class," she said. *Wow, what a Godsend!*

I was able to attend school for the next 3.5 years with that type of flexible job support. I worked five days and scheduled all my classes on my two days off. During the four years that I was in school, I remember my friends and family asking me when my next day off would be. "May 2017," I told them.

My first literature class at Kennesaw was "Black Women in Literature." I did not find out that it was a study of trauma until the first day of class. I was so glad to hear this because I knew that I would learn something that I could apply to my own life. Before taking this course, I had thought some of my past behavior was unusual. You see, I didn't start dealing with my mother's death until ten years after she passed. I didn't know it was typical; I thought I was a latent mourner. I truly had feelings around this and was surprised and extremely relieved to discover that my behavior was considered normal.

I had explained away my delayed grieving process by telling myself that I didn't have time for the pain and that grieving the loss of my mother would have been like saying I wanted her alive to continue suffering. However, Cathy Caruth argues that "trauma as it first occurs, is incomprehensible... the impact of the traumatic event lies precisely in its belatedness, in its refusal to be simply located" (Berger). Yes, yes, yes, it was a great moment of vindication! Thanks, Caruth.

I also experienced a defining moment during my first semester at Kennesaw. I had to reconcile within myself whether I was going to make it through college. I felt so foolish walking among all those young people on campus. Here I was old enough to be some of their grandparents and certainly old enough to be all of their parents. "What was I doing here?" I asked myself. It was a question I had to answer.

I found myself rationalizing that I

already had a family and raised my kids, and these young people hadn't done that yet. I further reasoned that I'd already been where they had to go. After resolving my doubts, I felt good. "Okay, I can do this," I said. That's how I answered the question and got through the next four years.

I also said to my son, "If you and I both stay on track, you'll graduate from high school in 2016, and I'll graduate from college in 2017." By the grace of God, that's what we did. My son, Alexander, graduated from North Springs High School in May, Class of 2016, and in the following year, I graduated from Kennesaw State University, Class of 2017. To God Be the Glory!

I received my Baccalaureate of Science Degree in Integrative Studies at the graduation ceremony on Wednesday, May 10, 2017. The entire day was surreal. The weather and graduation were perfect. I was so proud to be a graduate finally. Phillip and Alexander attended. Unfortunately, Anthony Jr. was not able to come, but my Aunt

Gracie and Uncle James were there as well as my brother Elliott and his wife. What a momentous occasion. I'm so glad they were able to share that special day with me.

About two weeks later, I had a graduation party to commemorate the occasion. The weather was perfect, and we enjoyed delicious food catered by Chef Poe. In attendance were my Pastor, Elizabeth Davis, the church Elders, and some of my closest friends from work, like Ms. Dot and Chantemekka. Also, two of my brothers, E l l i o t a n d T, their wives, two aunts, and a host of cousins were there.

I had a blast, and the gifts - just seemed to keep on coming. Even though my father was unable to attend, his gift blew me away. Thanks again, Dad, I'll never forget it. Everything was lovely. What a wonderful celebration and grand fulfillment of a long-forgotten dream.

Never Give Up! *"All things are possible to him that believeth"* (Mark 9:23b).

FINAL REFLECTIONS

I cannot overemphasize the role my faith played throughout my life. It was only because of my relationship with the Lord that I was able to survive the things that happened as I traveled *"The Road to Kennesaw."*

I went through hell a few times and came out on the other end. It is befitting for me to say, "I don't look like what I've been through." I knew this before a therapist told me these words as I began to explain why I felt the need for anti-depressant medication. He prescribed them for me, but I took the pills for less than a week and stopped. Instead, I went back to doing what I had been doing for the past 40 years. I nurtured my relationship with God, praying, reading my bible, singing, attending church, and listening to the Gospel radio station.

God was indeed my saving grace. I don't doubt for one minute that I would have been crazy or strung out on drugs had it not been for my relationship with Him. God knew that I was going to need Brother Frank long before He put him on my path.

Today, I stand in awe of my life: my travels, my strength, my faith, my accomplishments, my sons, and now my book.

What a momentous journey it's been. I spent so much of it merely trying to survive. But now, I feel like I can finally get on with the business of living.

"For I know the thoughts that I think toward you, saith the LORD, thoughts of peace, and not of evil, to give you an expected end."

– Jeremiah 29:11

MY PARENT'S LEGACY

James Edward and Annie Lou Giles Prayor

In response to why they continued to have children, my mother replied, "If a tree don't bear any fruit, then cut it down."

Momma was a strong and resilient woman. Despite being tormented by schizophrenia, she endured until her two oldest daughters were grown and out of the house. Momma gave birth to eight beautiful children, and although she died without seeing any of her grandchildren, her legacy continues to grow. We love you, Momma, and we look forward to seeing you again. Thank You!

As this book comes to print, I am so thankful that our Father is still with us. He is 89 years old and in better shape than all 10 of his kids. We love you Dad and Thank You for all you do!

As of April 2020, my parents have 23 Grandchildren and 10 Great-grandchildren.

To God Be the Glory!

"Children, obey your parents in the Lord: for this is right. ² Honour thy father and mother; which is the first commandment with promise; ³ That it may be well with thee, and thou mayest live long on the earth."

– Ephesians 6:1-3

ABOUT THE AUTHOR

Lois Prayor Williams is a motivational speaker, writer, and author. She currently lives in Atlanta, GA, along with her three sons. Lois ministers at her church, Reaps of Joy, in Decatur, GA.

Ms. Williams is currently working on an audiobook and is available for speaking engagements. You can contact Lois for bookings, comments, or inquiries at the following email address:

AuthorLoisWilliams@gmail.com.

(678) 851-1447

"Study to shew thyself approved unto God, a workman that needeth not to be ashamed, rightly dividing the word of truth."

– 2 Timothy 2:15

WORKS CITED

Andermahr, Sonya., Pellicer-Ortín, Silvia. *Trauma Narratives and Herstory*. Palgrave Macmillan, 2013

Beattie, Melody. *Codependent No More: How to Stop Controlling Others and Start Caring for Yourself*. Hazelden Publishing, 2009

Berger, James. "Trauma and Literary Theory" Contemporary Literature XXXVIII, 3, Board of Regents of the University of Wisconsin System, 1997

Bloom, Sandra L. M.D. "Trauma Theory Abbreviated." *Community Works*, October 1999

Caruth, Cathy. *Unclaimed Experience: Trauma, Narrative, and History*. John Hopkins University Press, 1996

Vickroy, Laurie, Korb-Khalsa, Kathy L., Azok, Stacey D., and Leutenberg, Estelle A. *Trauma and Survival in Contemporary Fiction*. University of Virginia Press, 2002

Made in USA - Crawfordsville, IN
53622_9780999425282
05.20.2020 2319